Animals of the Night

RIVER OTTERS AFTER DARK

Heather M. Moore Niver

Enslow Publishing
101 W. 23rd Street
Suite 240
New York, NY 10011
USA

enslow.com

Words to Know

carnivore—An animal that eats only meat.

extinct—No longer existing.

freshwater—Having to do with fresh water, not salt water or seawater.

habitat—The place in which an animal lives.

lens—Part of the eye that is clear.

mammals— Animals that have a backbone and hair, usually give birth to live babies, and produce milk to feed their young.

nocturnal—Mostly active at night.

pelt—The skin of an animal, usually with the fur, wool, or hair still attached.

predators—Animals that kill and eat other animals to stay alive.

prey—An animal hunted by another animal for food.

species—A group of the same kind of things, such as plants or animals, that have the same name.

Contents

Midnight Snack

All seems still in the night. But listen closely. There is a splash! A river otter is on the hunt. It dives headfirst into the pond. The water isn't too deep, so its tail is still above the water. Using its teeth and paws, the otter grabs a big fish!

Such a large meal needs to be eaten on land. The otter drags it to the shore with its teeth. After munching on a tasty midnight snack, the otter is ready for more. With another splash the otter is back on the hunt.

FUN FACT!

There are thirteen different species, or kinds, of otters. Eleven species live in freshwater, like the river otter. Two species live in the sea.

River otters sometimes snack right in the water if the meal is small.

Spotting an Otter

Otters are little **mammals** with thick brown fur. Most otters have round ears. Their legs are short and strong. They have small, slender bodies. Most are between 26 and 42 inches (66 and 107 centimeters) long. Their long, narrow tail is about one-third of its body. It is strong and muscular. Otters use their tails to help them swim and balance.

River otters love to live in the water. They are **nocturnal**. This means they are most active at night.

FUN FACT!

River otters are related to weasels.

Otters have webs between their toes. These are perfect for swimming!

If you hope to spot a river otter, you're in luck. River otters live all over the Americas, Europe, Africa, and Asia. They live in all kinds of habitats, too. River otters are found splashing around in freshwater, such as streams, lakes, reservoirs, and wetlands. Otters also live along oceans.

There must be lots of food to eat and water to swim in. An otter likes a home where there are plenty of places to hide. Piles of rocks, thick bushes, and leaves are ideal.

Otters usually live around eight or nine years in the wild. In safer habitats like zoos they can live for up to twenty-one years!

Otter Nosh

When it comes to dinnertime, the river otter is a carnivore. It likes its meat. Meals are mostly made up of fish, crayfish, crabs, mussels, and frogs. Sometimes otters eat turtles and other animals that live in the water. Other times they will happily eat a bird. River otters eat whatever prey they can get their paws on, though. They like a quick and easy supper, so their snacks might change during the year. They eat the animals that are available.

FUN FACT!

Sometimes otters are prey to larger animals, such as bobcats, alligators, and coyotes, as well as raptors like hawks and owls.

Freshwater otters like a fast meal.
They eat what's easy to catch.

River otters use their teeth and forefeet, or front feet, to catch their prey. Then they eat their meal. It doesn't matter if they are on land or in the water. Shallow waters are their favorite places to hunt. River otters are always hunting when they are in the water.

River otters use their whiskers to hunt, too. Whiskers are very sensitive. When the water currents move, they feel the vibrations with those whiskers. Prey may be swimming nearby!

FUN FACT!

Otters like to hunt slow-moving creatures that are easy to catch.

A river otter's whiskers help it hunt. They know a meal is nearby when they feel the water move!

Sensitive Otters

River otters have great senses. Their hearing, sight, smell, and touch are excellent. An otter finds other otters, food, and its home using its sense of smell. It also sniffs out **predators** that are near. Hearing is even more important when danger is nearby.

Sharp eyesight helps river otters look for food. They have special eyes for seeing underwater. The **lens** of their eye changes according to the light. So their sight is clear both under and above water. A good sense of touch helps otters find food in the mud.

An otter's nose and ears have a special way of closing when they dive into the water.

Slip-Sliding Away

It looks like otters have a whole lot of fun. They scamper on land. They slide down hills covered with mud, ice, or snow! Sometimes they land in the water with a splash! But this is more than play. It's a way to escape predators. When otters are on land, they run pretty well. They are much more at home in the water, though. A skilled slide into the water may help them get to safety much faster.

FUN FACT!

When they are on land, river otters move by running and jumping.

Otters like to have fun and play games with one another.

Pushy Mamas

Female river otters have between one and six babies at a time. Most of the time, they have just two or three. When it's time to give birth, the mother moves to an underground den. They usually have their young in the spring. The father otter does not help raise the babies.

Baby otters are completely blind when they are born. They need their mother's help with everything. At four weeks they start playing. And at eight to ten weeks they start to explore the world away from their usual playgrounds. By fall, otters are off on their own.

FUN FACT!

Male otters usually live alone. They hardly spend any time with the mother and babies.

Baby otters are called pups. They are born blind but are soon out playing with their siblings. This is how they learn the skills they will need to survive in the wild.

Baby river otters have to learn how to swim. Their mothers start teaching them to survive in the water when they are just two months old. Mothers don't gently help their young into the water, though. They push them in! But any otter is a natural swimmer. They figure out how to stay afloat pretty quickly. Soon they are swimming and splashing. River otters spend a whole lot of their lives living, playing, and swimming in the water.

Otter pups have to learn to swim quickly, because their mothers just give them a shove into the water! But because of their webbed toes and instincts, otter pups are natural swimmers.

Splish-Splash in the Water

Otters are at home in the water. They use their tails, strong back legs, and webbed toes to dart around underwater. Thick fur keeps the water away from their skin so they stay dry. This keeps them warm and toasty no matter where they are. Otters can stay underwater for up to eight minutes at a time. They can dive as deep as 60 feet (about 18 meters)!

FUN FACT!

Otters swim throughout the winter. They use holes in the ice to come up for air.

Otters have a long, strong body and powerful back legs and tail. These make it comfortable in the water.

Fussing Over Fur

During the day, the river otter spends some time taking care of its fur. But otters are not just worried about how they look! Otters work to keep their fur waterproof. Their fur does not naturally keep out water. Otters keep their fur glossy and oily by rubbing on logs and the ground. They use their paws to spread the oils and smooth their fur. Otters may spend almost half of their day working on keeping their fur ready for the water!

FUN FACT!

Otter fur has an oily surface. Underneath, the hair is very thick.

To stay warm and dry, otters oil their fur. This keeps it waterproof.

At one time, river otters were heavily hunted for their **pelt**, or fur. So many were trapped that they were almost **extinct** in more than twenty states. Many US states have worked hard to bring back otters. Today, otters are doing well in many areas.

But not all worries are over for otters. Sometimes they are still hunted. The clean water habitats get dirty from humans' garbage or poisons. They need fresh water to live and eat. As humans create more buildings, they use more land. They cut down trees. This means fewer leaves and plants for otters and other animals.

FUN FACT!

At the turn of the twentieth century, otter pelts were considered very valuable.

River otters are coming back from near extinction. Keeping Earth's waters and land clean will help them survive.

Otter Talk

Otters communicate in a few ways. Like most animals, they use their voices. Otters whistle, bark, snarl, and shriek. When they are scared or feel threatened, they make a "hah" sound. Otters may use touch or pose their body to show how they are feeling.

Sometimes otters want to leave a "note" behind when they are not there. They may rub their scent on objects. Other times they make "sign heaps." Otters make piles of grass, mud, or sand. This shows other otters where it has been.

FUN FACT!

Otters leave droppings behind, too. These are called "spraint."

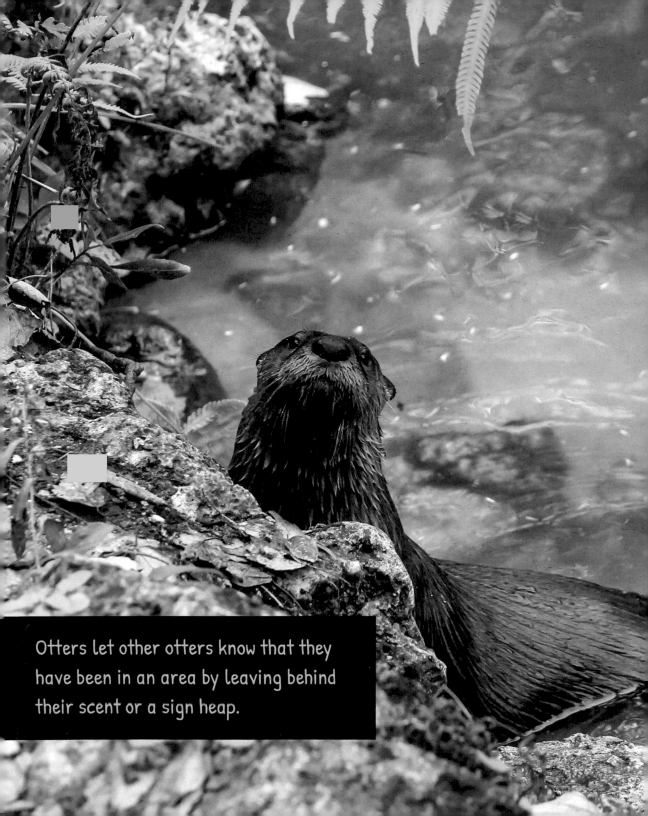

Otters let other otters know that they have been in an area by leaving behind their scent or a sign heap.

Stay Safe Around River Otters

- Don't approach or tease river otters. Is a river otter ignoring you? Good news. This means you are at a safe distance.

- Watch for changes in otter behavior. If the river otters change how they are acting, you might be too close. They will bite or attack if they feel threatened!

- Mothers with babies might be extra cautious. Keep your distance.

- Don't disturb the otter's surroundings. Remember, river otters leave piles of grass and other materials to communicate. Also, removing anything like these piles might not be legal in the area.

- Try to find a high place to watch river otters, such as a bridge or tree (if it's safe). Sit quietly. They cannot see things that are far away very well. They may not notice you.

Learn More

Books

Goldsworthy, Katie. *Otters*. New York: Weigl Publishing, 2012.

Swanson, Diane. *Otters*. Vancouver, BC: Whitecap Books, 2010.

Yoxon, Paul and Grace Yoxon. *Otters of the World*. Dunbeath, Scotland: Whittles Publishing, 2014.

Websites

San Diego Zoo: Otter

animals.sandiegozoo.org/animals/otter

Learn more about otters in rhe wild and in the zoo.

National Geographic Kids: River Otter

kids.nationalgeographic.com/content/kids/en_US/animals/river-otter

Check out facts, photos, and more about otters.

Watchable Wildlife: River Otter

www.dec.ny.gov/animals/6962.html

Head here for facts, photos, and links to videos about river otters.

Index

Published in 2017 by Enslow Publishing, LLC.
101 W. 23rd Street, Suite 240, New York, NY 10011

Copyright © 2017 by Enslow Publishing, LLC.
All rights reserved.

No part of this book may be reproduced by any means without the written permission of the publisher.

Library of Congress Cataloging-in-Publication Data
Names: Niver, Heather Moore, author.
Title: River otters after dark / Heather M. Moore Niver.
Description: New York , NY : Enslow Publishing, 2017. | Series:
Animals of the night | Includes bibliographical references and index.
Identifiers: LCCN 2015044853| ISBN 9780766077027 (library
bound) | ISBN 9780766077171 (pbk.) | ISBN 9780766076785
(6-pack)
Subjects: LCSH: North American river otter—Juvenile literature. |
North American river otter—Behavior—Juvenile literature. | Otters—
Juvenile literature.
Classification: LCC QL737.C25 N59 2016 | DDC 599.769/2—dc23
LC record available at http://lccn.loc.gov/2015044853

Printed in the United States of America

To Our Readers: We have done our best to make sure all website addresses in this book were active and appropriate when we went to press. However, the author and the publisher have no control over and assume no liability for the material available on those websites or on any websites they may link to. Any comments or suggestions can be sent by e-mail to customerservice@enslow.com.

Photo Credits: Throughout book, narvikk/E+/Getty Images (starry background), kimberrywood/Digital Vision Vectors/ Getty Images (green moon dingbat); cover, p. 1 Marka/UIG/Getty Images, samxmed/E+/Getty Images (moon); p. 3 Andrea Izzotti/ Shutterstock.com; p. 5 Matt Knoth/Shutterstock.com; p. 7 Steve Byland/Shutterstock.com; p. 9 chbaum/Shutterstock.com; p. 11 Kjersti Joergensen/Shutterstock.com; p. 13 David Dohnal/Shutterstock. com; p. 15 Kletr/Shutterstock.com; p. 17 © Weimann, Peter / Animals Animals — All rights reserved; p. 19 JeannetteKatzir/iStock/ Thinkstock; p. 21 Jule Lubick/Shutterstock.com; p. 23 l i g h t p o s t/ Shutterstock.com; p. 25 Tanya Puntti/Shutterstock.com; p. 27 S J Francis/Shutterstock.com; p. 29 Warren Price/iStock/Thinkstock.